Ten-Minute Grammar Grabbers

by Murray Suid

illustrated by Philip Chalk

This book is for
Leslie Kallen

Publisher: Roberta Suid
Editor: Carol Whiteley
Design and Production: Philip Chalk
Educational Consultant: Amy Dobry

Other Monday Morning publications by the author:
*Book Factory, For the Love of Research, How to Be an Inventor,
How to Be President of the U.S.A., Picture Book Factory, Report Factory,
Storybooks Teach Writing, Ten-Minute Editing Skill Builders,
Ten-Minute Thinking Tie-ins, Ten-Minute Whole Language Warm-ups*

ISBN 1-878279-99-8

Printed in the United States of America
9 8 7 6 5 4 3

CONTENTS

INTRODUCTION

Although the study of grammar goes in and out of fashion, most accomplished writers and editors agree on this: **Understanding grammar is a vital step in language mastery.**

The reason is simple: English is like a game. As with checkers, basketball, and other activities, players must know the rules and the jargon so that they can interact with the other players. This knowledge also makes possible self-evaluation.

What has this to do with grammar? Everything. *Grammar* is the name we give to the rules and definitions of language.

Learning to Love Grammar

No one would enjoy studying the rules of tennis but never playing the game. Likewise, studying grammar outside the context of reading and writing is a bore. But integrating grammar within the language arts can be interesting and even fun.

That's the idea behind *Ten-Minute Grammar Grabbers*. Through quick and easy projects, students learn sentence basics while using language creatively. These real-world applications include:
- composing mini autobiographies
- inventing titles
- giving directions
- hunting for language patterns in literature
- using the dictionary as a research tool
- writing stories that reinforce grammar concepts

How to Use This Book

Ten-Minute Grammar Grabbers is divided into two sections:

The first section, **Parts of Speech**, covers the basic terminology needed to analyze words as used in sentences. Students will discover how nouns, adjectives, verbs, and other forms of expression capture meaning.

The second section, **Sentences**, introduces the three main uses of sentences (stating information, asking questions, giving commands) and the various forms of sentences such as simple and compound sentences.

Throughout the book, each lesson features an activity that

takes only minutes to learn. You'll find a brief introduction plus step-by-step directions. In most cases, the only materials needed are paper and pencil. Frequently, the work can be done cooperatively in groups of two or three. If time permits, students can share their efforts in small groups or with the class.

Follow-up pages provide additional resources, for example, a sample dictionary page that prepares students for exploring real dictionaries. You'll also find models of the assignments, for example, a verb-focused biography.

Beyond Ten Minutes

Accompanying each quick activity is an extension project designed to expand student understanding of the given concept. These enrichment challenges lead to picture books, stories, reports, and other language arts creations.

Additional Resources

At the end of the book, you'll find a variety of materials used in many activities, for example, a list of sentence patterns, plus a simple method for diagramming sentences. The section features a reproducible "Grammar Guide" that students can refer to throughout the year. This guide includes definitions, examples, rules, and advice.

The Resources section also suggests strategies for teaching students learning English as a second language.

Where to Begin

The study of grammar doesn't have a clear beginning or ending. To understand verbs, you need to encounter nouns. To grasp sentence structure, you must be aware of sentence function.

This means that you can start anywhere. That's why the activities are listed in alphabetical order. However, those projects that appear early in the book introduce basic terms. Thus, if grammar learning is new to your students, you might wish to start with the first few activities.

A final hint: Each part of the book begins with a bulletin board that defines terms. If you put up such a board ahead of time, you'll find it handy for introducing concepts and later reinforcing them.

PART 1. PARTS OF SPEECH

English is a melting-pot language, enriched by people and cultures from around the world. One of the language's great strengths is its vast vocabulary, estimated at about a million words!

Amazingly, all these words—from "a" to "antidisestablishmentarianism"—fit into just eight basic categories. These are known as the "parts of speech." Each category represents a different way words are used to convey meaning. Once students grasp the eight fundamental parts, they'll be better prepared to incorporate new words they encounter.

The activities that follow are designed to make the eight parts of speech concrete. The bulletin board on the next page can set the stage for these activities. The idea is to represent visually the eight linguistic categories. You might point to the board when introducing one of the parts or when reinforcing the concept.

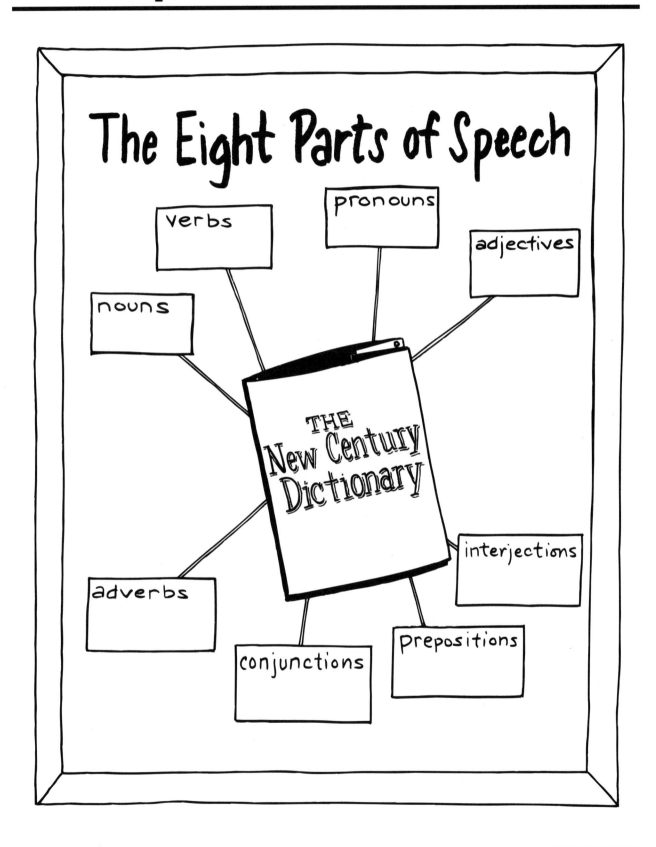

ALPHABETICAL GRAMMAR

The alphabet provides a familiar framework for brainstorming words that fit a part-of-speech category.

DIRECTIONS:
1. Choose one of the four most common parts of speech: noun, adjective, verb, or adverb. In this example, we'll use verbs.
2. Make sure students understand the part of speech by using a sentence frame:

I _____ a ball. (see, kick, catch, lost, etc.)

You'll find a collection of frames in "Resources" at the back of this book.
3. Have students try to find one verb for each letter of the alphabet. For example, the list of verbs might begin:

a	act
b	break
c	cry
d	dig

Students can brainstorm the words from their imaginations or by scouring a dictionary.
Note: "X" is always a problem with ABC activities. One solution is to let kids make up words. Another is to skip the letter, especially with the adjective and adverb categories.

EXTENSION:
Students can write and illustrate children's ABC books, each of which features a different part of speech. (See the models on the following page.)

From "ABC Nouns"

A is for Africa.

From "ABC Adjectives"

A is for acrobatic.

"I'm sorry."
A is for apologize.

From "ABC Verbs"

A is for awkwardly.

From "ABC Adverbs"

BIOGRAPHICAL WORDS

To paraphrase an old saying, "If the words fit, wear them."

DIRECTIONS:
1. Pick someone you are studying in class, or a kind of worker (painter, teacher, pilot, bus driver).
2. On the board, write a verb frame sentence for the person. This is a sentence that omits the verb, for example:

    A firefighter _____.
                 verb

3. Have the students brainstorm as many verbs as possible that fit the person.
4. If time permits—or later on—continue characterizing the person using different parts of speech:

    A firefighter should be _____.
                         adjective

    A firefighter needs a (an) _____.
                         noun

EXTENSION:
Have students create part-of-speech stories about themselves, friends, pets, or heroes. They can focus on one part of speech: "Five Nouns That Describe Eleanor Roosevelt." Or they can use several parts of speech. The significance of each key word should be explained by a sentence or paragraph. (See the model on the next page.)

Part-of-Speech Biography

Goldilocks' Verbs

Seven verbs are important in the story of "Goldilocks and the Three Bears."

walked: Goldilocks walked through the forest. If she had stayed at home, she wouldn't have gotten into trouble.

entered: Goldilocks knocked on the bears' front door but no one came to the door. She could have gone back home and that would have been the end of the story. But instead, she entered the house without permission.

ate: Goldilocks was hungry and decided to taste the three bowls of cereal. When she found cereal that was just right, she ate it all up. This upset the baby bear when he came home.

sat: Goldilocks was tired and sat in the three bears' chairs. She liked the baby bear's chair best and sat in it, but I guess she was too heavy because she broke it.

slept: After so much walking and eating and sitting, no wonder Goldilocks got tired. She tried out each bear's bed and found the baby bear's bed the best for her. She got in and slept.

screamed: When the three bears came home, they found all the damage that Goldilocks had done. When they found her, they woke her up and she screamed.

ran: Goldilocks' scream scared the bears. She ran out of the house and all the way home.

BOOKMARK REPORTS

Focusing on a single part of speech can lead to fresh insights into literature.

DIRECTIONS:
1. Ahead of time have students cut out bookmarks using lined paper. (See the model in the margin.)
2. Read aloud a short story, a picture book, or a poem.
3. Pick a part of speech—noun, verb, or adjective will work best. You might divide the class into three groups, each of which will work with a different part of speech.
4. Have students brainstorm words that fit the book and the word category. For example, verbs that fit "The Three Little Pigs" include: huff, run, chase, escape.
5. Students use one of their brainstormed words to title the bookmark. Then they write a sentence or two that previews or explains the story in terms of the key word. (See the models on the next page.)
6. The title of the book should go on the reverse side.
7. Share the bookmarks in small groups or post them.

EXTENSION:
Use the same word-focused approach to writing full-scale book reviews. For example, a paper about a book in the Great Brain series might be titled "Clever."

Bookmark Models

Escape, v.

"The Three Little Pigs" tells about three pigs who are almost eaten by the Big Bad Wolf.

The first pig builds a house of straw, which the wolf easily blows down. The pig escapes to the second pig's house, which is made of twigs.

When the wolf blows this house down, the two pigs escape to the third pig's brick house.

The wolf can't blow this house down. The pigs are safe and don't need to escape.

Dumb, adj.

"The Three Little Pigs" is a story about dumb characters.

One pig builds a straw house. That's dumb. A hungry wolf easily blows the house down.

The second pig is almost as dumb. He builds a twig house. The wolf quickly blows it down.

The third pig is not dumb. He builds his house out of bricks.

When the wolf can't blow this house down, he slides down the chimney, into a pot of boiling water. Now that's really dumb.

Bricks, n.

In "The Three Little Pigs," the first pig uses straw as a building material. The second pig uses twigs. Neither of these things is good when a huffing and puffing wolf is in the neighborhood.

The third pig understands that it's important to build a house out of something strong. He uses bricks. The wolf uses all his wind power, but he can't hurt this well-made house of bricks.

DICTIONARY HUNT

Rummaging through the dictionary is one of the best ways to reinforce understanding of the parts of speech.

DIRECTIONS:

1. Ahead of time prepare a dictionary hunt list. It can focus on one type of word, for example, proper nouns, or it can be mixed like the model on the next page. Of course, you needn't include the dictionary excerpt in a hunt list. Students can seek items by looking through a real dictionary.

2. Make sure students are familiar with the part-of-speech abbreviations used in the dictionary. A set of typical abbreviations appears on this page.

3. Have students, working alone or in small groups, fill in the sheet.

4. Share the results in small groups or on the board.

Abbreviations	
n.	= noun
adj.	= adjective
v.	= verb
adv.	= adverb
pron.	= pronoun
prep.	= preposition
conj.	= conjunction
interj.	= interjection

EXTENSION:

Have students create their own dictionary hunt lists to challenge their classmates or even the teacher.

Dictionary Hunt List

In the sample dictionary page below, find the following items:

1. A proper noun: _____

2. A pronoun: _____

3. A noun that can also be used as a verb: _____

4. An adjective with more than one meaning: _____

5. An interjection: _____

6. A noun consisting of two words: _____

---

hi, interj. A greeting.

I, pron. The person who is talking or writing.

ice cream, n. A frozen dessert made of cream.

icy, adj. 1. Made of ice. 2. Very cold. 3. Unfriendly.

if, conj. In the event that.

igloo, n. An Eskimo house usually made of blocks of ice or snow.

ill, adj. Not well.

in, prep. Contained by.

inch, n. A measure.
    v. To move slowly.

Indiana, n. One of the 50 U.S. states.

indigo, n. 1. A plant used to make a blue dye. 2. A blue dye made from indigo. 3. A dark blue color.

ink, n. A liquid used for writing or printing.
    v. To mark or color with ink.

FILL-IN STORIES

The following activity allows students to focus on parts of speech in the context of a story.

DIRECTIONS:
1. Prepare a story by deleting most or all of the adjectives. (See the model on the next page.) You can use ready-made stories including fables or jokes. Or use student-written stories.
2. Have students, working alone or in small groups, fill in the missing words. Their word choices can be humorous.
3. Share the stories orally or on a bulletin board.

Note: When repeating the activity, leave out words of a different part of speech, for example, verbs. Or leave out several types of words. In this case, label each blank with the missing part of speech so that students will get reinforcement as they complete the _____.

noun

EXTENSION:
Use fill-in story sheets to play a game, commercially known as "Mad Libs." The leader asks the audience to supply nouns, adjectives, and so on, without seeing the story. When reading back the story, the results are usually hilarious.

Adjective Fill-in Story

Fill in the missing adjectives. You'll need to change "a" to "an" if you use an adjective starting with one of the five vowels: a, e, i, o, or u.

Jack was a _____ boy who lived with his _____ mother in a _____ cottage. The only _____ thing they owned was a _____ cow. One day, Jack's mother told him to sell the cow for food money. Jack was _____ because he loved the _____ cow. But he obeyed his mother and led the cow toward the _____ town not far from where they lived.

On the way the _____ boy met a _____ stranger carrying a _____ sack. The stranger took a few _____ beans from the sack and said, "If you give me your cow, I'll give you these magic beans." Jack couldn't resist the word "magic" and went ahead with the _____ trade.

When Jack showed his mother the beans, she became _____ and threw them out the window. The _____ morning, when he went outside, Jack saw a _____ sight. There was a _____ beanstalk that reached the _____ sky. Excitedly, Jack climbed the beanstalk and came to a _____ castle owned by a _____ giant. When Jack heard the giant's _____ words—"Fe, fi, fo, fum"—the boy slid down the _____ beanstalk, which he then cut down with a _____ axe.

GRAMMAR FLIP BOOK

Why should Hollywood actors have all the fun? Here's a "motion picture" activity in which words get to star.

DIRECTIONS:

1. Ahead of time, assemble a flip book. You might use the model on the next page. Duplicate it on thick stock or glue a copy onto tagboard. Cut out the panels and staple them as a book.
2. Demonstrate the flip book to your class.
3. Give each student six note cards cut in half to make 12 panels. (The number is arbitrary.)
4. Have the students choose an action that can be illustrated by a simple object in motion. Some examples:

blink: An eye closes and opens.
bounce: A ball hits the ground and bounces.
crash: Two cars or trains run into each other.
draw: A pencil draws a line or shape.
drip: A faucet emits a drop of water.
fall: An object falls from a table.
jump: A person or animal leaps over a barrier.
roll: A ball rolls down a hill.
shake: Two hands intertwined move up and down.
smile: Lips turn upward into a smile.
wave: A hand moves back and forth.

5. Students draw the object at the beginning of the action, then make a series of drawings on the rest of the panels in which the object moves just a little each time. *Note:* A stationary part of the picture should be drawn in the same place each time, for example, a flagpole.
6. Staple the drawings into a book, and flip the movie.

EXTENSION:

Use the same technique to illustrate other parts of speech. For adjectives, a small ball might become big, or a black and white car become red. A preposition flip book might show a figure moving into a circle.

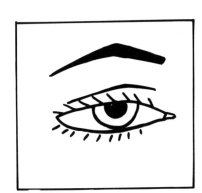

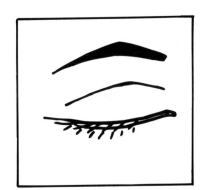

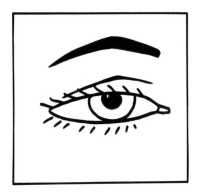
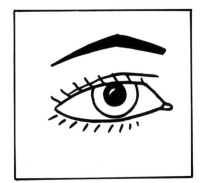

GRAMMAR GRAPHING

Who says math and language arts don't mix? Here's a graphing activity that reinforces understanding of the eight parts of speech.

DIRECTIONS:
1. Assign each student or team a page in a dictionary.
2. Review the dictionary's part-of-speech abbreviations, for example, "n." for "noun." (See page 14.)
3. Have them use tally marks to count the number of nouns, adjectives, and so on.
4. Students should rank the parts of speech by frequency: which appears most often, which appears the second most often, and so on.
5. Share the results to see if all the teams found the same rankings.

EXTENSION:
Have students make simple bar or pie graphs of the data. Each graph should name the source of the words counted as in the model on the next page. Later, you might create a class-wide graph that pools the data collected by all the students.

nouns ⅷⅷⅷⅷ|||| pronouns ||

verbs ⅷ || conjunctions

adjectives ⅷ| prepositions |

adverbs |||| interjections |

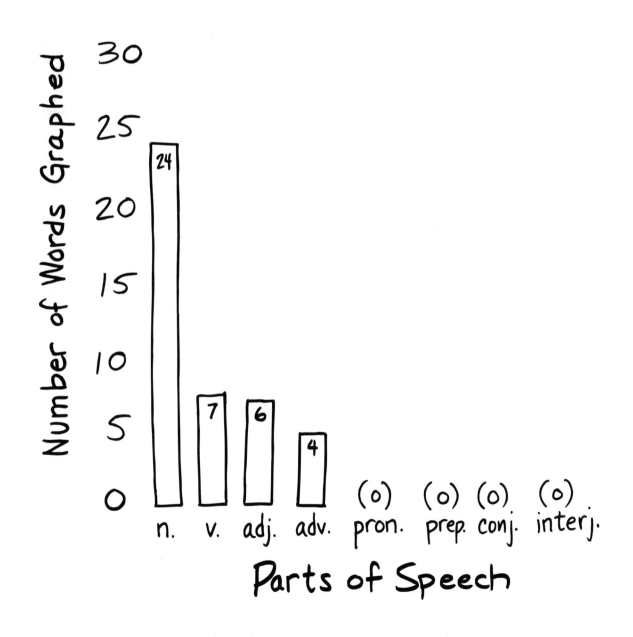

Graph of
Dictionary Page 184
(gl<u>ue</u> to g<u>oble</u>t)

HEAD HUNTING

Newspaper headlines (called "heads" by journalists) are a rich source for word study. Using headlines in a grammar lesson has an extra benefit: It may interest students in reading the newspaper.

DIRECTIONS:
1. Ahead of time collect a large number of newspaper headlines.
2. Divide the class into small groups and give each group a pile of headlines.
3. Students should glue or staple interesting headlines onto sheets of paper and label each part of speech in the headline. When in doubt, students should refer to the reproducible "Grammar Guide" (see "Resources") or check the part of speech in the dictionary. The goal is to find at least one example of each type of word.

EXTENSION:
Create a "Parts of Speech" bulletin board featuring newspaper headlines. (See the next page for ideas.)

Words in the News

adj.   v.

Large earthquake rocks Japan

n.   p.n. (proper noun)

adv.   verb   noun   verb   adj.

How to train your cat to act like a dog

prep.   adj.   prep.   prep.   noun

Can you figure out
each part of speech in this headline?

?   ?

Mayor says, "I quit"

?   ?

LIFT FOR ANSWERS

LABELING WORDS

The following activity sharpens dictionary skills while reinforcing the concept of the parts of speech.

DIRECTIONS:
1. Give students famous sayings, for example, "Two heads are better than one." (You'll find a list of sayings in "Resources.")
2. Students should use a dictionary to determine the part of speech of each word in the saying. *Note:* In many cases, a word will fit more than one category. For example, store is a noun when it means "building," and a verb when it means "to keep."
3. Share the results orally or by having students create grammar hang-ups. (See the model below.)

EXTENSION:
Do the same activity with a fable, joke, student story, or other short piece. To start, students copy the text, skipping every other line. Next, they identify each word's part of speech. (See the model on the next page.) The dictionary will come in handy for making sure that the words are correctly labeled. Finally, bind the pages into a grammar-teaching story book.

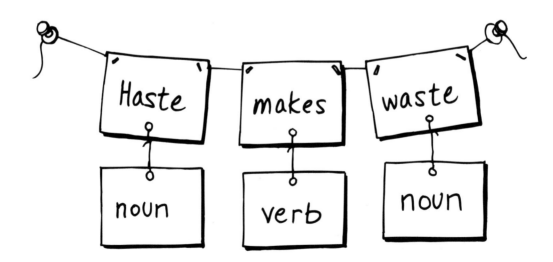

Labeled Story

The Fox and the Grapes

adj.   n.   adv.   adj.   adj.   n.   v.   prep.   adj.   n.   prep.

Many years ago, a hungry fox went into a vineyard in

n.   prep.   n.   adj.   n.   v.   n.   prep.   adj.   n.

search of food. The fox saw bunches of beautiful grapes

prep.   adj.   n.   adj.   n.   v.   prep.   pron.   n.   conj.   pron.   v.

in the vines. The fox stood on his toes, but he could

adv.   v.   adj.   n.   adv.   pron.   v.   conj.   adj.

not reach the grapes. Next he jumped, but the

n.   v.   adv.   prep.   n.   adv.   adj.   n.   v.

grapes were still beyond reach. Finally, the fox found

adj.   n.   conj.   v.   prep.   v.   adj.   n.   adv.   adj.   n.   conj.

a stick and tried to knock the grapes off the vine, but

adj.   n.   v.   adv.   adj.

the stick was too short.

pron.   v.   adv.   v.   adj.   n.   adv.   v.   adj.   n.

"I do not want the grapes anyway," said the fox.

pron.   v.   adv.   adj.

"They are probably sour."

MULTIPURPOSE WORDS

Many words in English can be used in two or more ways. For example, "boost" can function as a verb and as a noun. Making students aware of this verbal flexibility can give their vocabularies a boost.

DIRECTIONS:

1. To introduce the notion of flexibility, ask students to brainstorm as many uses as they can for a newspaper (something to read, a hat, a sunscreen, a wrapper, a mat to sit on if the grass is wet, papier-mâché, a protective floor covering when painting, etc.).

2. Explain that some words also have multiple uses. Demonstrate this by writing two sentences on the board, showing a single word used two ways:

> I found a shoe. (noun)
> I need a shoe box. (adjective)

Remind students that a word's part of speech depends on its use in a sentence.

3. Give students several multipurpose words and have them write sentences using each pair in different ways. (A list of such words appears on the next page.)

EXTENSION:

Have students go through the dictionary looking for words that can be used in two or more ways. Make a bulletin board of these multipurpose words. Include sentences that show each word being used as different parts of speech.

Multipurpose Words

Use each of the following words as two different parts of speech. Label each one as in the example.

```
             noun                    verb
              |                       |
bank: I went to the bank.    Today, I will bank the money.
```

bike	need
butter	number
button	paper
catch	pitch
comb	play
cook	ride
count	rip
cure	safe
cut	shout
dance	sip
drink	smile
drive	smooth
fall	staple
fish	study
flock	talk
glass	tape
help	walk
hike	watch
hit	water
joke	wave
laugh	win
mail	wish

PANTOMIME THE PARTS

Drama is an involving way to help students understand the concept of parts of speech.

DIRECTIONS:
1. Choose a part-of-speech category to act out. Verbs are a good place to start.
2. Assign each student a word to pantomime. (*Note:* Some words, like "converse," may require two actors.) Depending on the class's level of sophistication, the verbs can relate to simple actions, such as "eat" and "stir," or more subtle behaviors, such as "forget" and "think."
3. After each student or team pantomimes the word, classmates should guess what it is.

EXTENSION:
To build vocabulary, assign words that are new to the students but which have familiar synonyms, for example, "ingest/eat." When called on, a student writes the "new" word on the board, pronounces it, and mimes it as classmates try to guess its meaning. (The word list on the next page includes optional acting tips for students.)

"New" Verbs to Pantomime

Verbs	Acting Tips
catapult (throw)	Throw an imaginary object.
circumvent (bypass)	Walk around a stool or other object.
commence (start)	Begin in a frozen position, then start an action.
contemplate (think about)	Scratch head, look at the sky, etc.
decamp (leave)	Get up from a chair and exit.
don (put on)	Put on an imaginary garment.
elude (avoid)	See something and move in the other direction.
encounter (meet)	Two actors meet.
endeavor (try)	Try to do something, e.g., fly an imaginary kite.
enlighten (tell about)	One actor gestures to another who "gets it."
eschew (avoid)	One actor avoids another actor.
explicate (explain)	One actor tells another how something works.
expunge (erase)	Erase an imaginary word on the chalkboard.
guffaw (laugh)	Pretend to laugh.
immerse (dip)	Dip hands in imaginary dishwater.
impede (block)	One actor blocks the path of another.
masticate (chew)	Pretend to chew a bite of a sandwich.
nictate (wink)	Wink.
perambulate (walk)	Stroll.
peruse (read)	Read an imaginary newspaper.
procure (buy)	One actor mimes buying something from another.
quaver (tremble)	Pretend to shake from fear.
remunerate (pay)	One actor pretends to pay another for something.
replicate (copy)	Copy something from a book.
respire (breathe)	Breathe slowly and deliberately.
ruminate (think about)	Pretend to think about something.
saunter (walk)	Take a leisurely walk.
savor (enjoy)	Pretend to eat something with pleasure.
wrest (pull)	Two actors try to pull an object from each other.
writhe (twist)	Squirm in a painful way.
yearn (want)	Desire something that's just out of reach.

PICTURE THE PARTS

Students don't have to be Rembrandts to illustrate the concept of each part of speech. They just need imagination.

DIRECTIONS:
1. Choose the part of speech you want students to visually define.
2. Brainstorm a list of examples of this part of speech and list the words on the board. Assign each student a word.
3. Suggest a strategy for picturing the given part of speech:
- adjective—draw one object many ways
- noun—draw many objects
- verb—draw many actions
- preposition—draw one object in many places (in a box, on a table, under a car, etc.)
- conjunction—for "and," show pairs of things; for "or," show two things on a branching road
- interjection—draw people excited, angry, afraid, etc., and add dialogue balloons

The concepts of adverb and pronoun are tricky to illustrate, but maybe your gifted students will come up with a way.

4. Have students sketch their ideas and add a caption that names and defines the part of speech. (See the model on the next page.)
5. Share the ideas in small groups or on a bulletin board.

EXTENSION:
Create a class-made picture grammar book that defines all the parts of speech.

striped cat

furry cat

fat cat

playful cat

Adjectives add details to nouns. They answer questions like "What kind?" or "How many?"

RIDDLE WORDS

This part-of-speech guessing game provides practice in observation and imagination.

DIRECTIONS:
1. Choose a part of speech to focus on. In this example, we'll use the verb category.
2. Ahead of time, the leader—teacher or student—creates a part-of-speech riddle. This task requires:
• Choosing an "answer" word, which the other players will try to guess, for example, "do."
• Writing at least three clues that use the mystery word.

For example:

       I _____.

       _____ you know how to spell balloon?

       _____ the right thing.

See the next page for additional model riddles.
3. When play begins, the leader says the first clue aloud, or writes it on the board. To keep the game going, it's best to start with the least obvious clue.
4. If no one can figure out the riddle, the leader gives another clue.
5. When players think they know the answer, instead of shouting it out they should suggest another clue, for example, "_____ you know the way to San Jose?"
6. After all the clues have been given, the leader asks the players to guess the word.

EXTENSION:
Create individual or small-group-created whole-class riddle books in which the front of each page lists the clue words and the reverse page gives the answer.

Model Riddles

Adjective Riddle

_____ shoulder
A _____ spell
It's usually _____ in the winter.
The ice was _____ .
     (Answer word: *cold*)

Preposition Riddle

_____ a minute
_____ trouble
_____ a hurry
_____ luck
_____ hot water
     (Answer word: *in*)

Adjective Riddle

_____ sauce
_____ water
The _____ air balloon rose quickly.
It's usually _____ in the summer.
     (Answer word: *hot*)

Preposition Riddle

_____ the rainbow
head _____ heels
Jack jumped _____ the candlestick.
     (Answer word: *over*)

Conjunction Riddle

Life, liberty, _____ the pursuit of
     happiness
Beauty _____ the Beast
Green Eggs _____ Ham
soap _____ water
     (Answer word: *and*)

Pronoun Riddle

_____ do you want?
_____ is wrong?
I know _____ happened.
     (Answer word: *what*)

Noun Riddle

Will you shake my _____ ?
Give me a helping _____ .
At noon the big _____ is on the 12.
Put your right _____ over your heart.
     (Answer word: *hand*)

Verb Riddle

_____ where you're going.
_____ out.
_____ closely.
_____ your step.
     (Answer word: *watch*)

SIMON SAYS

This old party game is a high-energy way to boost interest in the parts of speech.

DIRECTIONS:
1. Review the game rules: A leader gives the other players a task to do, but the listeners do it only if the leader first announces: "Simon says." Followers who perform the action without hearing "Simon says" must sit down.
2. Choose a category of words. The game works especially well with adverbs, adjectives, and prepositions.
3. Each student prepares a list of directions for the category. This can be done ahead of time. (See several models on the next page.)
4. The leader, standing in front of the followers, who also stand, rapidly gives directions, sometimes deliberately omitting "Simon says."

EXTENSION:
Make a class book of Simon Says scripts, which students can share with other classes or take home to play with their parents.

Simon's Sayings

Adverbs (These must be presented with verbs.)

Simon says:
wave slowly
eat sloppily
applaud enthusiastically
move gracefully
chew happily
stand nervously
draw carefully
dress quickly

Adjectives (Include a linking verb, for example, "look" or "seem.")

Simon says look:
happy
sad
friendly
silly
smart
mean
afraid
nervous
lost
confused

Prepositions (Present each as part of a prepositional phrase.)

Simon says put your hand:
on your head
on your other hand
over your heart
under your chin
against your cheek
over your eyes
near your elbow
behind your knee
into your pocket

SUBSTITUTIONS

Revising a story can reinforce grammar concepts while building vocabulary and dictionary skills.

DIRECTIONS:
1. Ahead of time find a story or essay and underline all the instances of a given part of speech, for example, all the adjectives. The lines will facilitate follow-up discussion. (See the model on the following page.)
2. Make sure students understand which part of speech they'll be working with. Then have them go through the worksheet, replacing the underlined words with synonyms. Encourage the use of the dictionary or thesaurus.
Note: When you're working with verbs, students might change the tense of each verb instead of finding synonyms.
3. Students can share their rewritten versions orally in small groups or by posting them.

EXTENSION:
Have students create additional worksheets for classmates to revise or to take home to try with their parents.

36

Change the Adjectives

Replace each underlined adjective with another adjective that makes sense. Write the new adjective above the old one.

The Hare and the Tortoise

1   One day, a <u>conceited</u> hare, who thought he

2   was <u>better</u> than everyone else, met an <u>old</u> tortoise.

3   "You are so <u>slow</u>," said the <u>nasty</u> hare.

4   "I'm not as <u>fast</u> as you," said the tortoise, "but I get

5   where I'm going."

6   "Let's race," said the hare, who thought this would be a

7   <u>good</u> time to show off.

8   The tortoise agreed and the <u>exciting</u> race began.

9   The hare was so far ahead of the tortoise that when

10   he reached the halfway point he said to himself, "I'm

11   <u>sleepy</u>. I'll take a <u>quick</u> nap and then finish the race."

12   While the hare slept, the tortoise kept going. He passed

13   the <u>dreaming</u> hare but didn't say a word.

14   When the hare woke up, the tortoise was far ahead. It was

15   the <u>persistent</u> tortoise who crossed the finish line first.

16   The fable teaches an <u>important</u> lesson: Slow and steady

17   wins the race.

TITLE CREATIVITY

An exciting title can unleash a writer's energy. Who wouldn't want to create stories to go with *The Runaway Bunny, Where the Wild Things Are,* or *Tuck Everlasting?*

DIRECTIONS:
1. Choose a part of speech.
2. On the board, list at least five words that fit the given category. For example, if you chose prepositions, your list might be:

       in
       inside
       near
       behind
       against
       under

3. Have students, working alone or with partners, brainstorm as many titles as they can that start with one or more of the words. For example:

       Inside the Pencil Sharpener
       Behind the Tall Tree
       In a Swimming Pool One Day
       Behind the Mask
       Under My Pillow

4. If time permits, or later on, have students write stories, poems, or essays to go with their titles.

EXTENSION:
Have students collect titles that feature a given part of speech or a pattern. Then have students create their own versions. For example, *The Cat in the Hat* (noun phrase, prepositional phrase) could lead to:

       The Bicycle in the Mud Puddle
       The Bird at the Window
       The Sandwich in My Stomach
       The Cloud Over the School

Other patterns are given on the next page.

Title Patterns

Here are classic patterns that students can look for. Note that there will be overlaps. For example, any title with a prepositional phrase will also fit the "title with a noun" category.

Titles with Proper Nouns
Constance
Pocahontas
Sara, Plain and Tall
Strega Nona
The Island of the Skog
The Tale of Peter Rabbit

Titles with Adjectives
The Amazing Bone
Curious George
Green Eggs and Ham
The Little House on the Prairie
The Red Balloon

Titles with Verbs
The Dark Is Rising
The Day Jimmy's Boa Ate the Wash
Horton Hatches the Egg
The Stupids Step Out
Why Mosquitoes Buzz in People's Ears

Titles with Prepositional Phrases
The Cat in the Hat
Tales of a Fifth Grade Nothing
There's a Nightmare in My Closet
The Wonderful Wizard of Oz

Titles with Conjunctions
Alexander and the Terrible, Horrible, No Good, Very Bad Day
And to Think That I Saw It on Mulberry Street
But Not the Hippopotamus
Charlie and the Chocolate Factory
Mike Mulligan and His Steam Shovel

"WANTED" WORDS

English grammar is about patterns. For example, to form the simple past tense, you usually add "ed" to the present verb. There are, however, irregularities such as sing, sang, sung. One way to handle these grammar "troublemakers" is to shine a creative spotlight on them.

DIRECTIONS:
1. Choose an irregular form to work with:
• verb forms, for example: see, saw, seen
• plurals, for example: hoof, hooves
2. Write a few regular examples on the board to make sure students understand the typical pattern.
3. Give each student, or student team, an irregular word to study using the dictionary. You'll find a list of irregular verbs and a list of nouns with irregular plurals in "Resources."
4. Have students create wanted posters that warn unwary writers and speakers about these verb or noun "villains." Each poster should illustrate the correct but irregular pattern of the "wanted" word. (See the model on the next page.)
5. Display the posters around your room or around the school.

EXTENSION:
Create a book of wanted posters for "Verb Villains."

WANTED

"Eat"

If you see this word, be careful. It has an irregular past tense and an irregular past participle:

> I eat.
> I ate.
> I have eaten.

Do not confuse this word with "chew," "devour," "swallow" or other words that relate to eating. These words are regular:

> I chew.
> Yesterday, I chewed.
> I have chewed.

WORD OF THE DAY

Everyday experiences can easily become part of your grammar program.

DIRECTIONS:
1. Ahead of time, post a "word of the day" chart. It should list the eight parts of speech.
2. At the end of the day—or end of the period—have students brainstorm a word that sums up their experience in the classroom. The brainstorming might be open to all words, or it could be limited to a specific part of speech.
3. The class can vote for one word or—to avoid having a popularity contest—you could drop the ballots into a hat (or any other "voting machine") and pick a winner.
4. Write the word on a note card, date it, and clip it to the appropriate part of speech.
5. Duplicate the Word Calendar (next page). In the box at the top, write in the name of the month and number the days. You might have students take turns adding art to the box.
6. Each day, enter a word of the day in the small date box.

EXTENSION:
At the end of the month, choose a word that represents the most important event of the month, and write it in the "word of the month" box at the bottom of the calendar.

Word Calendar

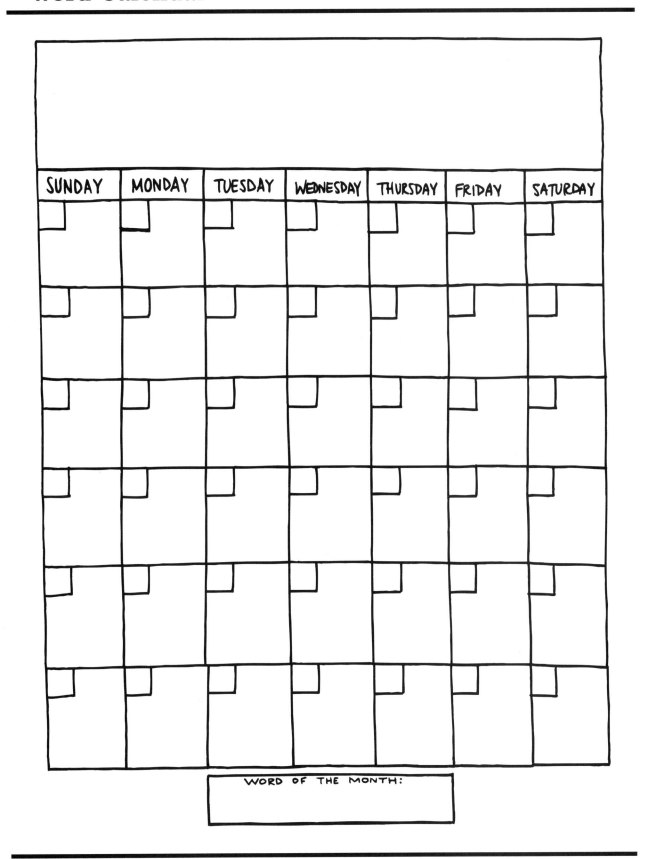

SUNDAY	MONDAY	TUESDAY	WEDNESDAY	THURSDAY	FRIDAY	SATURDAY

WORD OF THE MONTH:

WORDS IN THE WORLD

The following observation activity relates grammar to the students' environment.

DIRECTIONS:
1. Choose a part of speech on which to focus. The noun is a good starting point.
2. Ask students to look around the room and list the nouns that name everything in sight.
3. Share the lists orally or by posting them.
4. Later, repeat the activity for other parts of speech. For verbs, students can list the actions that go with the objects they see:

        sit in a chair
        draw on the chalkboard
        locate a place on the map
        call the office on the intercom

Adjectives can be listed with nouns:

        wooden floor
        torn shade
        square desk

EXTENSION:
Have each student draw a familiar place, for example, a room at home, and label each noun in the picture. (See the model on the next page.)

Nouns in My Living Room

bird cage

clock

window

tree

bird

door

family picture

doorknob

fireplace

telephone

umbrella

lamp

chair

mug

magazine

log

fire

table

rug

plant

sofa

PART 2. SENTENCES

The sentence is the main building block for stories, essays, reports, and many other kinds of writing. Strong sentences inform, delight, teach, convince, thrill, and tickle readers.

The practices in this section are designed to efficiently sharpen sentence-writing skills. Sentence study deals with two topics: function and structure. The first three lessons in this part of the book focus on three fundamental sentence functions:
• providing information (declarative sentences)
• giving commands (imperative sentences)
• asking questions (interrogative sentences)
The rest of the section deals with structure: how sentences are put together. Using easy activities such as matching and filling in, students become familiar with the key elements found in all sentences: subjects and predicates. Follow-up activities lead to exploring and using classic patterns such as the simple sentence and the complex sentence.

An important lesson—Sentence Repairing—uses editing and revising practice to reinforce a variety of grammatical concepts.

To start, you might create a "Sentence Basics" bulletin board (see next page) that defines terms and serves as a continuing reference guide to all that follows.

DECLARATIVE SENTENCES

Creating an autobiographical reference book can be a powerful way to practice writing declarative sentences.

DIRECTIONS:
1. Make sure students understand what a declarative sentence is: a sentence that states a fact or an opinion.
2. Have each student write as many declarative sentences as they can about themselves:

> My name is Murray.
> I'm ten years old.
> I have a brother.
> My dog has fleas.
> I can play the saxophone.
> I know how to use a computer.

Advanced students can divide their declarative sentences into two lists—facts ("I'm 1.5 meters tall") and opinions ("My dad makes the best pizza in town").
3. Have students spend a few minutes in small groups sharing the news about themselves.

EXTENSION:
Students can write declarative-sentence autobiographies or biographies in the form of picture books—featuring one sentence per page. See the model on page 49.

family
hobbies
pets
skills
travels

I like to play basketball.

I'm interested in astronomy.

The scariest thing I ever did was jump off a three-meter diving board.

IMPERATIVE SENTENCES

Although most writing consists of declarative sentences, imperative sentences play a role in writing directions, for example, "How to Use a Microscope." Imperatives also are useful when writing dialogue.

DIRECTIONS:
1. Make sure students are familiar with the structure of the imperative. Write a few examples on the board, pointing out that imperatives usually begin with a verb:
• Chew carefully.
• Keep off the grass.
• Play it again, Sam.
2. Duplicate the map on the next page and have students, working alone or with a partner, write directions that would lead a person from one end of the town to the other.
3. Later, repeat the activity by having students write a series of imperative sentences that tell how to get from the classroom to their homes or to some other location in town.
4. Share the directions aloud or on the board.

EXTENSION:
Have students give directions for carrying out an activity. It can be something simple, like making a bed, or something complicated, like practicing a new song on the piano.

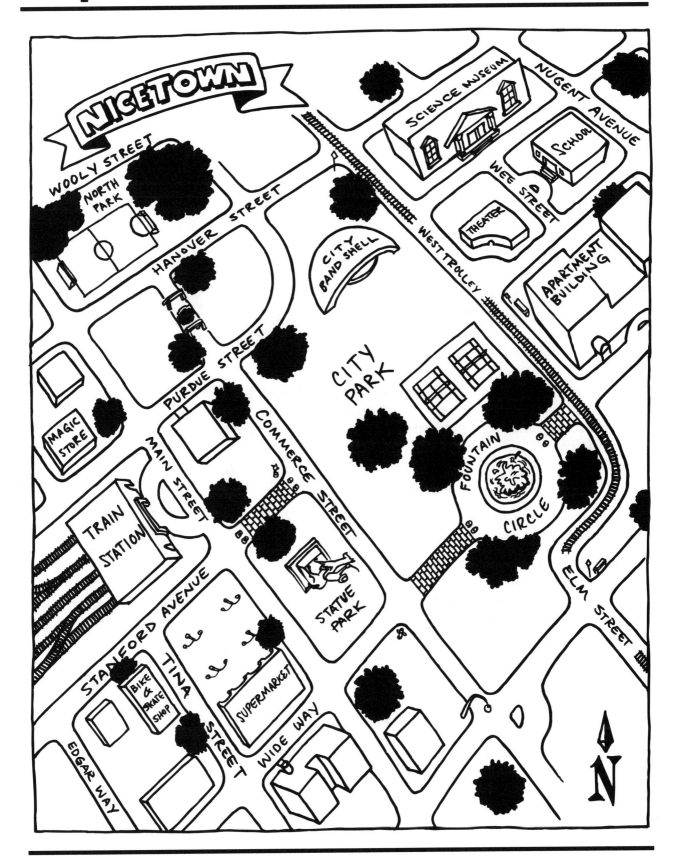

INTERROGATIVE SENTENCES

Understanding question sentences ("interrogatives") is not only part of grammar mastery. Scientists, writers, and artists regard questions as vital to creativity. That's why students should become "question machines."

DIRECTIONS:

1. If necessary, review the two fundamental structures of question sentences:
- Helping verb + subject + main verb:
    - Will you sing?
    - Can we play?
- Interrogative pronoun + verb:
    - Who laughed?
    - What happened?

2. Pose a topic students are familiar with, or show them a picture that evokes questions. (See the next page.) Alternatively, have students choose their own topics: the moon, soccer, stamp collecting, scouting, or cats.

3. Students then generate as many questions as possible about the topic. These can be questions that the students can already answer or questions they would like to be able to answer.

4. Have students share their questions. Later, they might use the questions as research starters.

EXTENSION:

Have students further hone their questioning skills via two classic question-based activities:

- Self-interviews—writers interview themselves about an area of expertise (see the model on page 54).

- Twenty Questions—a leader picks a mystery topic (a famous person, an invention, a living thing, etc.) and gives the class a clue: it's animal, vegetable, or mineral. The class then asks up to 20 questions to solve the mystery. You can introduce the game by reading aloud a transcript (see page 55). Or just play it with the class and see what happens.

How does it grow? Is it good for you? How many kinds are there? How does it make you cry? Why does it make you cry?

Self-interview Model

A Scary Car Crash

Last week my mom and I were in an accident. To tell the story, I've asked myself a few questions.

Q: Do you feel like talking about the accident?

A: Yes.

Q: What happened?

A: We were going shopping. My mom was driving. I was next to her. When we came around a curve, we saw a car stopped in front of us.

Q: Why had it stopped?

A: The owner said he had run out of gas.

Q: What happened next?

A: My mom slowed. Then a car crashed into us from behind.

Q: Did you get any warning that you'd be hit?

A: We heard a screech when the driver put on the brakes.

Q: Were you hurt?

A: I had a broken rib. My mom's face was bruised. Luckily, we both had our seat belts on.

Q: What happened to your car?

A: It was a total wreck. That's because after it was hit, it was pushed into the car in front of us. Now we'll have to get a new car. Maybe we should get a tank.

Sample "Twenty Questions" Game

Leader: The subject is "animal."

Q 1: Is it a person?   Leader: No.

Q 2: Is it an animal in a story?   Leader: Yes.

Q 3: Is it in a children's book story?   Leader: Yes.

Q 4: Does it have fur?   Leader: Yes.

Q 5: Does it talk?   Leader: No.

Q 6: Is it the main character?   Leader: Yes.

Q 7: Does its name appear in the title?   Leader: Yes.

animal

Q 8: Are there people in the story?   Leader: Yes.

Q 9: Do the people like the animal?   Leader: No.

Q 10: Does the animal bite people?   Leader: No.

Q 11: Does it wear clothes in the story?   Leader: Yes.

mineral

Q 12: Is it a dog?   Leader: No.

Q 13: Is it a cat?   Leader: No.

Q 14: Is it a monkey?   Leader: No.

Q 15: Does it walk on four feet?   Leader: Yes.

Q 16: Does it make a well-known noise?   Leader: No.

vegetable

Q 17: Can it be a house pet?   Leader: Yes.

Q 18: Is it a rabbit?   Leader: Yes.

Q 19: Is it Peter Rabbit?   Leader: Yes.

SENTENCE COUNTING

One cause of run-on sentences is lack of awareness. Students get caught up in the flow of stories, and don't realize that prose consists of separate sentences. A simple way to increase sentence awareness is having students count sentences in all sorts of writing: newspaper articles, picture books, and other publications.

DIRECTIONS:

1. Give each student a piece of writing with between five and twenty sentences. Several ready-to-use examples appear on the next page. But you might also use short newspaper articles, fables, jokes, or excerpts from longer works.

2. Have the students count the number of sentences in the piece of writing.

3. Share and discuss the results. Note that a sentence that contains another sentence—for example, a quotation—is counted as one sentence.

EXTENSION:

Give students writing assignments with a set number of sentences, for example: "My Birthday Party Described in Seven Sentences" or "Buttering a Piece of Toast Described in Four Sentences."

Wow! There are ten sentences on this page!

My Cat in Four Sentences
My cat Hush is more than a pet. About a dozen fleas live happily in her fur. I do almost everything I can to chase them away, but they always come back. I guess they like her as much as I do.

How Many Sentences?

Galileo's Discoveries

No one knows for sure who invented the telescope. We do know that an Italian teacher named Galileo was one of the first scientists to use a telescope for astronomy. In 1609, Galileo studied the moon using a simple telescope. He made several famous drawings that showed that the moon had mountains and craters. Galileo later observed that Jupiter has several moons. Until then, scientists believed that the Earth was the only planet that had a moon.

An Accident That Became a Toy

The Slinky is one of the most popular toys ever. Yet, it wasn't invented by a toy maker. Richard James was an expert with springs. One day, in his lab, he accidentally knocked over a spring. He was amazed by the way it did somersaults. He didn't think it had any value until he told his wife Betty about it. She immediately recognized that this was something children would love to play with. In 1946, the couple started a company, which now sells a million Slinkies a year.

Squeeze It

Until 1892, dental cream was sold in jars. People in a family would dig their toothbrushes into the same jar before brushing. This method seemed unsanitary to a dentist named Washington Sheffield. Dr. Sheffield knew that soft foods had been packaged in collapsible tubes. He thought the same method would work for dental cream, and it did. Today, we call the product "toothpaste."

The Most Popular Song in the World

Can you name the song that's sung most often throughout the world? You've probably sung it many times yourself. The song is: "Happy Birthday to You." The familiar melody was written in 1893 by two sisters, Mildred and Patty Hill. They were teachers who used the song—then titled "Good Morning to You"—to greet their students. A few years later, the sisters changed the words to "Happy Birthday to You." Although the Hill sisters are dead, the song is still considered private property, and every time it's used on TV or in a movie, the song owners get paid.

SENTENCE ELEMENTS

Knowing how to identify subjects and predicates is essential for dealing with subject-verb agreement problems (page 78), run-on sentences (page 79), and sentence fragments (page 80).

DIRECTIONS:
1. Write a simple sentence on the board. Underline the complete subject once and the complete predicate twice. Circle the simple subject, which is usually a single word.

    The two **birds** flew in a circle.

Explain that every sentence consists of at least one subject and one predicate. Define "subject" as "who or what the sentence is about." Define "predicate" as "what the subject is or does." Every predicate includes a verb, which usually is the first word in the predicate.
2. Write another sentence on the board. Have students copy it and underline the complete subject once or circle the simple subject, and underline the predicate twice. To make sure students correctly analyze the sentence, do the work yourself on the board.
3. Repeat this activity frequently to reinforce the concept. (See the next page for sample sentences to use.)

EXTENSIONS:
Here are four more ways to teach sentence structure:
• Matching: Have students match subjects and predicates from a ready-made list. (See page 60.)
• Filling in: Write a subject on the board, and have students brainstorm as many predicates as they can that work with it. Similarly, write a predicate on the board, and have students brainstorm subjects that fit. (You'll find lists of sentence starters on pages 61 and 62.)
• Analyzing: Give students double-spaced stories or articles and have them identify subjects and verbs in each sentence. (See the sample on page 63.)
• Diagramming: This old activity still works. (See a simplified label-and-arrows method on page 94.)

Identifying Subjects and Predicates

A **chain** is only as strong as its weakest link.

A hungry **stomach** cannot hear.

A rolling **stone** gathers no moss.

A small **hole** can sink a big ship.

A **stitch** in time saves nine.

All **sunshine** makes a desert.

An empty **sack** cannot stand up.

Birds of a feather flock together.

Haste makes waste.

The **leopard** can't change his spots.

Little **strokes** fell great oaks.

Lost **time** is never found again.

People who live in glass houses shouldn't throw stones.

Rome wasn't built in a day.

Still **water** runs deep.

Talk does not cook rice.

Two **heads** are better than one.

You can't judge a book by its cover.

Matching Subjects & Predicates

Match each subject with a predicate that makes sense. In some cases, more than one predicate will match a subject.

Subjects	Predicates
1. A big cloud	A. happens just once a year.
2. The stolen bicycle	B. was thunder.
3. Laughter	C. is to pick it up.
4. Fresh baked bread	D. made a shadow in our yard.
5. A fork	E. knows everything.
6. A secret	F. should follow orders.
7. My wish	G. can be like a friend.
8. The loud noise	H. is found around the world.
9. A birthday	I. can help keep you healthy.
10. A robot	J. can be hard to keep.
11. A good book	K. is not useful when eating soup.
12. Learning to exercise	L. was found this morning.
13. Nobody	M. has a wonderful smell.
14. The best way to eat corn	N. came true.

Add the Missing Predicates

Add a predicate to complete each sentence. The predicate includes a verb and any words that go with the verb.

Two and two _____

The sun _____

Swimming _____

The best way to fall asleep _____

Television _____

The ocean _____

A playful kitten _____

I found _____

The noise _____

Long ago, dinosaurs _____

Everyone _____

A scary dream _____

A good book _____

A rainbow _____

Lying _____

Your nose _____

Add the Missing Subjects

Add a subject to complete each sentence. The subject is
"who" or "what" does the action.

_____ move quickly.

_____ smiled at me.

_____ fell down.

_____ doesn't happen every day.

_____ woke me up.

_____ can be dangerous.

_____ is a good way to make friends.

_____ costs more than $100.

_____ shouldn't scare you.

_____ have many uses.

_____ come in several colors.

_____ should be kept in the refrigerator.

_____ makes some people laugh.

_____ do not exist.

_____ is a waste of time.

_____ bothers me.

_____ is one thing animals can't do.

_____ is somewhere I'd like to visit.

Find the Subjects and the Verbs

Underline the subject of each sentence. Then put two lines under the verb that goes with it. The first sentence has been marked for you.

The Story Behind the Slinky

1. <u>The Slinky</u> <u><u>is</u></u> one of the most popular toys in history. The

2. story of its invention may surprise you. This popular plaything

3. was not invented by a toy maker.

4. The Slinky's inventor was Richard James. Mr. James was an

5. expert with springs. He was working in his lab one day when he

6. accidentally knocked over a spring. He was amazed by the

7. result. The spring acted like an acrobat. One end flew over

8. the other again and again.

9. Mr. James didn't think the spring had any value until he told

10. his wife Betty about it. Betty James immediately recognized that

11. this was something children would love to play with. She called

12. the toy "Slinky." The word "slinky" means sneaky. Mrs. James

13. thought the spring moved in a sneaky way.

14. In 1946, the couple started a company to make Slinkies. The

15. company is still in business and sells about a million Slinkies

16. each year.

SENTENCE FORMS

You can help students become familiar with sentence forms by having them complete incomplete "sentence starters."

DIRECTIONS:
1. Choose a sentence form that you want students to practice, for example, the complex sentence. (See pages 91-93 for a list of sentence forms.)
2. Write two or three examples on the board to make sure students understand the pattern.
3. Write a sentence starter on the board, for example:

      If I saw a flying saucer, _____.

See the next three pages for a variety of sentence starters.
4. Have students, working alone or with partners, complete the sentence in as many ways as possible. Encourage creativity and humor.

      If I saw a flying saucer...

            I'd wave at it.

            I'd run away.

            I'd know I was dreaming.

            you'd be the first to know about it.
5. Share the results on the chalkboard.

EXTENSION:
Have students write a book of sentence starters to be used by other classes.

Sentence Starters

The following examples are based on the list of sentence patterns found in "Resources" at the back of this book. These starters can be endlessly varied. For example, you can use little twists, such as "Put the sentence into the past tense." Or you might specify the number of words to add.

Simple Sentences

Add the predicate (one verb):

Every day, I _____.

My friend _____.

Add a compound predicate (two verbs):

I _____ and _____ every day.

The squirrels _____ and _____.

Add a single direct object:

I saw a _____.

Who found the _____?

Add a compound direct object (two direct objects):

I need _____ and _____.

The car smashed into a _____ and a _____.

Add a single predicate adjective (an adjective describing the subject):

Today, you seem _____.

This book is _____.

Add three predicate adjectives that describe the subject:

My friend is _____, _____, and _____.

The elephant is _____, _____, and _____.

Sentence Starters

Simple Sentences (continued)

Add a single predicate noun (a noun that defines the subject):

A banana is a _____.

A school is a _____.

Add the verb to form an imperative sentence:

_____ to the store.

_____ this book.

Add a single subject:

_____ doesn't scare me.

_____ is something everyone enjoys.

_____ will make people smarter.

Complete the compound subject:

_____ and _____ are winter activities.

_____ and _____ make an interesting sandwich filling.

_____ and _____ are two important inventions.

_____ and _____ are not easy to understand.

Compound Sentences

Complete the second clause:

I'll play my saxophone, and you _____.

Today is my friend's birthday, but _____.

You can paint pictures, or you _____.

Complete the first clause:

_____, or you can do it.

_____, but don't tell me about it.

_____, and my friend wants to eat pizza.

Sentence Starters

Complex Sentences

Complete the independent clause:
Because I like to swim, I _____.
If you want to become President, you _____.
Until you say you're sorry, I _____.

Complete the introductory subordinate clause:
Although _____, they didn't win the race.
When _____, I laughed.

Complete the sentence-ending subordinate clause:
I didn't wake up because _____.
She won't say anything unless _____.
That dog became a hero when _____.
You can borrow my coat if _____.
I'm afraid of flying on airplanes although _____.

Complete the "who" clause:
That stranger is someone who _____.
I need a friend who _____.
Anyone who _____ will want to read this book.

Complete the "which" clause:
The red car, which _____, was stolen.
The storm, which _____, caused much damage.

Complete the "that" clause:
I saw a movie that _____.
They were looking for a boat that _____.
This magazine article says that _____.
I can't believe that my sister _____.

SENTENCE MAKING

Here's a fun way to give students practice in manipulating the parts of a sentence.

DIRECTIONS:
1. Choose a type of sentence: declarative (statement), interrogative (question), or imperative (command).
2. Ahead of time, prepare lists of the different elements that form the given kind of sentence. (See the samples on the next three pages.)
3. Write the items on the board or duplicate as worksheets.
4. Have students, working alone or in small groups, mix and match the parts to create unusual sentences. The results may be silly, but the sentence structure should be solid.
5. Share the sentences orally.

EXTENSION:
Have students create their own build-a-sentence resource sheets, and then exchange them with partners.

Declarative Sentence Machine

Build a sentence by choosing any subject from Column 1,
any verb from Column 2, any direct object from Column 3,
and any prepositional phrase from Column 4.

Use the same method to create more sentences.

Column 1 (subjects)	Column 2 (verbs)	Column 3 (direct objects)	Column 4 (prepositional phrases)
The tigers	lost	money	under water.
My friends	ate	mud	on the roof.
Your cousins	wore	bananas	in a boat.
The firefighter	needed	shoes	with a smile.
Their robot	found	smoke	through the night.
A French poodle	made	music	near the lake.
A lonely carrot	heard	mustard	behind the tree.
Nobody	saw	TV	beyond the wall.
Everybody	wanted	alligators	until yesterday.
The moon	remembered	a promise	between the cars.
Superman	chased	nobody	before noon.
The cowboy	smelled	the rain	along the shore.

Imperative Sentence Machine

An imperative sentence is a sentence that tells someone to do something. For example: "Keep off the grass."

Build an imperative sentence by choosing any verb from Column 1, any object from Column 2, and any adverb from Column 3.

Use the same method to create more sentences.

Column 1 (verbs)	Column 2 (objects)	Column 3 (adverbs)
Take	the rocket	now.
Stop	the chicken	never.
Photograph	the books	tomorrow.
Buy	the ocean	quickly.
Wash	the elephant	cheaply.
Cheer	your hat	later.
Study	the floor	softly.
Sell	the joke	secretly.

Interrogative Sentence Machine

An interrogative sentence asks a question. For example, "Can you hear me?" Most interrogative sentences begin with a helping verb—for example, "will" or "do."

Build an interrogative sentence by choosing any helping verb from Column 1, any subject from Column 2, any adverb from Column 3, and so on.

Use the same method to create more sentences.

Column 1 (helping verbs)	Column 2 (subjects)	Column 3 (adverbs)	Column 4 (verbs)	Column 5 (objects)
Do	you	always	believe	stories?
Will	your cats	often	say	signs?
Are	those ants	usually	remember	noodles?
Aren't	my ears	never	chew	advertise-ments?
Won't	those cars	quickly	dig	poems?
Don't	people	eagerly	write	pigs?
Can	buffaloes	slowly	draw	hats?
Can't	friends	quickly	fold	puppets?

SENTENCE REPAIRING

Chalkboard editing practices reinforce grammar concepts while sharpening the skills needed for revising actual assignments.

DIRECTIONS:
1. Choose a problem to work on. Focus on a problem that occurs in your students' writing or choose one of the problems described on the next page.
2. On the board, write a sentence that illustrates the problem, for example, a run-on sentence such as:

      I play the piano my teacher's name is Sandy

3. After mentally editing the sentence, students write a corrected version in their notebooks. They might discuss the changes they made with a partner.
4. Edit the sentence on the board so students can check their work and make additional corrections if needed.

      I play the piano. My teacher's name is Sandy.

5. To reinforce the concept, repeat the exercise using different sentences. You'll find lists of ready-to-edit material in the "Resources":

- Subject-Verb Agreement Problems (page 78)
- Run-on Sentences (page 79)
- Sentence Fragments (page 80)
- Tense Errors (page 81)

EXTENSION:
For a more realistic editing simulation, give students handouts featuring longer editing practices. Use a variety of formats, such as stories and letters. Number the lines to facilitate discussing the problems after the students have marked the worksheets. (See pages 82 and 83.)

Note: Ten-Minute Editing Skill Builders (Monday Morning Books, 1996) offers a year's worth of chalkboard and paper edits.

Four Major Sentence Problems

Run-on Sentences (See page 79 for editing practices.)
Just as words thatruntogether confuse readers, sentences that lack clear beginnings and endings are hard to follow. There are three causes:
• Omitted punctuation and capitalization: "The dog barked the cat meowed."
• Comma used for a period (comma splice): "The storm raged, I trembled."
• Too many "ands" (stringy sentence): "I fell off my bike and it hurt and I..."
Hint: Having students read their work to a partner can help them recognize and fix run-on problems.

Sentence Fragments (See page 80 for editing practices.)
Every well-made sentence consists of a subject and a predicate. If a group of words lacks a subject or a predicate, it's called a sentence fragment. Results in awkward, hard-to-understand writing. (You just read a sentence fragment! Did it jar you?) While sentence fragments should usually be expanded into complete sentences, there are a few exceptions. Titles are often sentence fragments (*The Wizard of Oz*). So are many exchanges in dialogue:

"What's going on?" I asked my friend.
"Nothing."

Still, students should learn to recognize and repair unintended fragments.

Subject-Verb Agreement Problems (See page 78 for editing practices.)
Subjects and verbs must agree in number. This means that if the subject is singular, the verb must be singular. If the subject is plural, the verb must be plural. For most verbs, the singular and plural are the same except for the third person singular (he, she, it).

	Singular	Plural
First person	I walk.	We walk.
Second person	You walk.	You walk.
Third person	He walks.	They walk.

Irregular verbs vary from this pattern—I <u>am,</u> you <u>are,</u> he <u>is</u>—and require extra practice, especially for students speaking English as a second language.

Tense Troubles (See page 81 for editing practices.)
While most English verbs form the past tense by adding "-ed" to the present, some frequently used verbs have irregular past-tense forms. A common error resulting from this is using the past particle (for example, "seen") for the past ("saw"), or using non-standard forms ("brang" for "brought").

GRAMMAR GUIDE

Adjective: A word that describes a thing: "a red ball."
A **comparative adjective** compares two things. It usually ends in er: "This fish is bigger than that one."
A **superlative adjective** compares one thing with two or more others. It usually ends in est: "That's the biggest fish here."

ball

Adverb: A word that tells how, where, or when an action occurs. Most adverbs end in ly: "Run quickly." A few adverbs, such as "very," work with adjectives: "a very happy teacher."

striped ball

Agreement: The matching of words that work together. For example, the subject of a sentence must agree with its verb in number. A singular subject needs a singular verb: "Mary laughs." A plural subject needs a plural verb: "We laugh."

Article: One of three special adjectives—"a," "an," or "the." "A" and "an" mean the same thing, but "an" is used in front of words that start with vowels—a, e, i, o, u—or vowel sounds: "an apple," "an hour."

Clause: A sentence that is part of another sentence: "You won because you tried harder."

Conjunction: A word that joins words: "I swam and biked." "You went to the party but I didn't." "I'll eat when I'm hungry."

Contraction: A shortened word or a word formed from two other words by omitting some letters: "can't" is a contraction of "cannot"; "don't" is a contraction of "do not." Because "do" is a verb, and "not" is an adverb, "don't" is a combination verb-adverb.

Declarative sentence: A sentence that states a fact or an opinion: "That building has ten floors." "It's hot today."

Direct object: The thing that receives the action of a verb: "I hit the ball." "Who lost the book?"

Helping verb: A verb that works with a main verb, indicating the time or likelihood of an action: "I will sing." "I might sing."

Imperative sentence: A sentence that gives a command: "Be quiet." "Turn left." In most imperative sentences, the subject is omitted but understood to be "you": "(You) keep off the grass."

Interjection: A word that shows surprise or emotion. Interjections are often punctuated with an exclamation mark: "Wow!"

Grammar Guide

Interrogative sentence: A sentence that asks a question and ends with a question mark: "Who is there?" "Why did you do that?"

Hint: A question can be a good way to start a report: "Who really discovered America?" Questions also make good titles.

Noun: A word that names a person, place, thing, activity, idea, or feeling. "The twins in the brick house had a bad dream about snow."

A proper noun names a particular person, place, or thing: Cleveland, Mars, Abigail. Proper nouns are capitalized. All other nouns are called common nouns.

Hint: Use exact nouns. Instead of "The magician did a neat thing" it would be clearer to write: "The magician did a neat trick."

Paragraph: One or more sentences working as a unit. The first line of a paragraph is usually indented—moved a short space to the right.

Part of speech: One of the eight categories into which all words fit: adjective, adverb, conjunction, interjection, noun, preposition, pronoun, and verb. Each type of word does a different job. For example, nouns label things, whereas verbs label actions.

Passive-voice sentence: A sentence in which the subject receives the action instead of creates the action: "The football was kicked by me." The verb in a passive-voice sentence is formed by combining a helping verb (is, was, were, etc.) with the past particle.

Hint: Your writing will often be clearer if you replace the passive voice with the active voice. Instead of "I was chased by you" try "You chased me."

Person: One of three groups of pronouns.

First person pronouns identify the writer or speaker: I, me, we, us, etc.

Second person pronouns identify the individual being addressed: you, your, etc.

Third person pronouns identify individuals or things spoken about: he, she, it, him, her, they, them, etc.

Phrase: Two or more words that work together, at times as if a single word or part of speech.

A **noun phrase** usually contains one or more adjectives and a noun: "I saw the red barn."

Grammar Guide

A **prepositional phrase** usually contains a preposition and a noun: "I went to school."

A **verb phrase** contains a verb and an adverb: "ran quickly."

Plural: More than one. The plural of most nouns is formed by adding s or es to the singular: car, cars; box, boxes.

Possessive noun: A noun that shows ownership. With most nouns possession is shown by adding apostrophe + s to the singular form—"The girl's book"—and apostrophe to the plural—"The girls' club."

Possessive pronoun: A pronoun that shows ownership: your, his, hers, our, their. Some dictionaries label these words as adjectives.

Predicate: The part of a sentence that contains the verb. In the simplest kind of sentence, the predicate and the verb are the same thing: "I sang." But a predicate can contain many words. In the following example, the predicate is underlined: "I <u>sang an old song about a frog who wanted to fly in a rocket to the moon.</u>"

Preposition: A word that shows spatial relationships. Examples include: in, on, near, over, under. Prepositions usually appear in prepositional phrases: "It's on the table." "It's in the water."

Pronoun: A word that can replace a noun. "This is a good book. I like it." There are dozens of pronouns. These include: I, you, he, she, it, we, us, they, and them. The word that a pronoun replaces is called the antecedent of the pronoun.

Hint: Repeat the antecedent (noun) from time to time so that the reader will understand to what the pronoun refers.

Sentence: A group of words that makes sense by itself. A sentence always contains a subject (what or who the sentence is about) and a verb (the action of the subject). In the following example, the subject is underlined once, and the verb is in boldface letters: "<u>Birds</u> **fly**." The part of the sentence containing the verb is called the "predicate" of the sentence. There are three major sentence forms:

Simple sentences consist of one subject and one predicate: "The grass is green."

Compound sentences contain two or more simple sentences, joined by a comma and a conjunction (and, but, or): "You are my friend, and that makes me happy."

Grammar Guide

Complex sentences consist of two sentences joined in a way that makes one sentence explain the other: "I ate because I was hungry." "Study until you learn the lesson."

Hint: Watch out for **sentence fragments,** word groups that are punctuated like sentences but which lack a subject or a predicate. Also, avoid run-on sentences made from two sentences that should be separated.

Subject of a sentence: What the sentence is about. In this example, the subject is underlined: "My friends play soccer."

Hint: For clarity, usually put the subject early in the sentence.

Tense: When an action occurs. Tense is usually indicated by the form of the verb. There are many tenses. Six important types are:
• simple present: "Today I laugh."
• ongoing present: "I'm laughing."
• simple past: "I laughed."
• ongoing past: "I was laughing."
• indefinite past: "I have laughed."
• future tense: "I will laugh."

Hint: Your writing will be clearer if you use one tense throughout a paragraph, or even throughout an entire piece of writing.

Verb: A word that labels the action in a sentence: "I listen." If the action of the verb relates to an object, the verb is called a **transitive verb** and the object is called the direct object: "I threw the ball."

Verbs change their forms to create different tenses. The forms are: present, present participle, past, and past participle. With most verbs, known as "regular verbs," the past and past participle are the same.

present	present participle	past	past participle
walk	walking	walked	walked

Irregular verbs use different patterns and can cause problems.

present	present participle	past	past participle
eat	eating	ate	eaten
go	going	went	gone

Hint: If you're unsure about the form of a verb (for example, the past tense of bring), look it up in the dictionary.

EDITING PRACTICE

Agreement

In these chalkboard practices, the correct verb is in parenthesis. The hints are mini-lessons to share with students.

1. My neighbor never say (says) a word to me.
Hint: Note that the singular form of the third person present tense verb almost always ends in s. This may seem odd because s signals the plural of most nouns.

2. Three birds sits (sit) on a fence.
Hint: Remind students that the plural form of the present tense verb does not add an s. We play, jump, etc.

3. We was (were) in the library when the fire broke out.
Hint: The verb "to be" (am, is, was, etc.) is tricky and may require a great deal of practice.

4. There is (are) many reasons for you to study.
Hint: Although this sentence begins with "There," the subject is "reasons," which is obviously plural. Identifying the subject is crucial in establishing subject-verb agreement.

5. There's (There are) three whales swimming toward shore.
Hint: "There's" may sound OK, but the contraction equals "There is," which sounds wrong and which is grammatically wrong.

6. No one have (has) arrived yet.
Hint: Think "not one."

7. One of my "friends" are (is) coming for dinner.
Hint: While friends is plural, it is not the subject of the sentence but rather part of a prepositional phrase ("of my friends") which describes the subject. The subject here is "One," which is clearly singular.

8. The band are (is) playing a popular song.
Hint: While a band consists of more than one person, because it functions as a unit, it is treated as a singular subject. The same would be true for a sentence like "The class is going on a trip."

Editing Practice

Run-ons

Basic run-ons: To fix these, add a period at the end of the first sentence and capitalize the first word of the second sentence, or rewrite the two sentences as one sentence.

1. Seven months have thirty-one days the first is January.

2. Bamboo is a kind of grass its hollow stem has many uses.

3. Insects have six legs because spiders have eight legs, they aren't insects.

4. Curling is game played on ice players use brooms to move a stone toward a target called a "tee."

5. Some words imitate sounds in nature an example is the word "crash."

6. Mexico City is one of the world's largest cities about eight million people live there.

7. English is related to German it is spoken in more than 60 countries.

8. There are two kinds of blood cells one is red and the other is white.

Comma splices: To fix these, end the first sentence with a period and capitalize the first word of the second sentence, or rewrite as one sentence.

1. Ice is a solid form of water, it forms at zero on the Centigrade scale.

2. You probably know that the plural of "goose" is "geese," you may not know that the plural of "mongoose" is "mongooses."

3. March is named for Mars, he was the Roman god of war.

Editing Practice

Fragments

There are many ways to convert these fragments into complete sentences. For example, "A big explosion" might become:

I heard a big explosion.
A big explosion won't scare me.
We expected a big explosion.

1. A big explosion.

2. Walking into town one day by myself with nothing to do.

3. Laughing and singing.

4. Smashed right into the wall.

5. Very exciting movie.

6. Something strange.

7. In the house that stands on the hill near town.

8. An awful sound.

9. Until it happens.

10. If you don't believe me.

Examples 11-15 involve merging fragments to form a complete sentence. Sometimes, a word or two must be added.

11. A promise. Should be kept.

12. There were flowers. As far as you could see.

13. We had fun on our vacation. Biking, singing, and other activities.

14. The honking horns. We couldn't sleep.

15. This is my best friend. Sandy.

Editing Practice

Tense Errors

1. They been away on vacation.

2. I awaked early yesterday.

3. I begun to take music lessons last year.

4. The letter carrier brang our mail early today.

5. The storm come a day early.

6. At the party I drunk too much soda.

7. The bird gone south for the winter.

8. The baby grown a lot this year.

9. Because I felt dizzy, I laid down for a while.

10. I was late so I run all the way to school.

11. I seen a movie last Friday.

12. My shirt shrunk when I washed it.

13. I swum all the way across the lake.

14. I wroted an e-mail letter to my friend.

15. While playing baseball, I catched three fly balls.

16. We sung "Happy Birthday to You" to our teacher.

Editing Practice

Mixed Errors

Note to the teacher: An uncorrected version appears on page 83. Students can simply cross out errors and write in corrections above the cross outs. Alternatively, you might teach a few standard editing marks, illustrated in the margin.

You may discover that students find different ways to solve problems. This variety proves that editing is an art.

/o = delete

∧ = insert

t̲̲ = capitalize

G̶ = make lower-case

⊙ = add a period

Keep Your Eyes Open

1   People often wonders where inventors gets their ideas.

2   One place is nature! The invention of the airplane are a

3   good example.

4   Hundreds of years ago Leonardo da Vinci studies birds.

5   He used what he learned to sketch ideas for building flying

6   machines unfortunately he never did build one.

7   Centuries later, a bicycle maker named Wilbur Wright

8   spent many hours on his back! Studying birds through

9   binoculars. Wilbur noticed that the birds raised and

10   lowering their wings whenever they turn this discovery led

11   to the invention of a kind of airplane wing that could

12   change its change when the pilot wanted make a turn. The

13   new wing, patented in 1906, makes human flight possible.

14   Many other inventors were inspired by things which

15   they see in nature. If you keep your eyes open, you may

16   make a new discoveries yourself.

Editing Practice

Editor's name: _____ Date: _____

Keep Your Eyes Open

1   People often wonders where inventors gets their ideas.

2   One place is nature. The invention of the airplane are a

3   good example.

4   Hundreds of years ago Leonardo da Vinci studies birds.

5   He used what he learned to sketch ideas for building flying

6   machines unfortunately he never did build one.

7   Centuries later, a bicycle maker named Wilbur Wright

8   spent many hours on his back. Studying birds through

9   binoculars. Wilbur noticed that the birds raised and

10   lowering their wings whenever they turn, this discovery led

11   to the invention of a kind of airplane wing that could

12   change its change when the pilot wanted make a turn. The

13   new wing, patented in 1906, makes human flight possible.

14   Many other inventors were inspired by things which

15   they see in nature. If you keep your eyes open, you may

16   make a new discoveries yourself.

SAMPLE FRAMES

Nouns

A noun is the name of a person, place, thing, activity, idea, or feeling. The answer to "who" or "what" usually is a noun.
    Examples: What are you looking at? A cloud. A tree.

Singular nouns name one instance of a group of things.
    Examples: A girl. A boy. A bike. A cat. A class.

A (An) _____
My _____
Give me the _____.
Over the _____
I'll trade you a (an) _____ for a (an) _____.

Plural nouns name more than one instance of a group. Plural nouns usually end with the letter s or the letters es.
    Examples: Two girls. Two boys.

Show me two _____.
Several _____ appeared on TV.
I don't need a thousand _____.

Proper nouns—as opposed to "common" or "ordinary" nouns—name a specific member of a group. The name distinguishes that member from all others. For example, "singer" is a common noun naming a type of performer. Frank Sinatra is a proper noun naming a specific singer. Proper nouns are almost always capitalized.
    Examples: Theodore, Cleveland, the Titanic.

_____ is a city (state, country) that I would like to visit.
If I could have dinner with any person, it would be _____.

Sample Frames

Adjectives

An adjective is a word that names an attribute (a quality) possessed by a person, place, or thing. The attribute can relate to something physical (color, size, texture, condition) or to a value (goodness, worth).

Simple adjectives focus on one person, place, or thing.

I found a (an) _____ book [ball, bird, key, shirt, bicycle].
This was a (an) _____ test.

Comparative adjectives establish a relationship between one person, place, or thing and another. These adjectives are usually formed by adding er to the simple adjective.
        Example: I am taller than you.

I am _____er than my friend [than a dog, a rocket, etc.].
A cat is _____er than an ant [a whale, a house].

Comparative adjectives may also be formed by changing a final y to i, then adding er: furry, furrier.

Superlative adjectives state that a person, place, or thing has more of the given quality than all other persons, places, or things in a given category. These adjectives are usually formed by adding est to the simple adjective.
        Example: I am the coldest person here.

That house is the _____ building in town.
Your plan is the _____ idea I ever heard.

Superlative adjectives may also be formed by changing a final y to i, then adding est: happy, happiest.

Special attention should be given to two adjectives that have irregular forms: good, better, best; and bad, worse, and worst.

Sample Frames

Verbs

There are two kinds of verbs: action verbs and linking verbs.

An action verb tells what someone or something is doing.
    Examples: The chorus sang a song. The tree fell on a car.

I _____ the ball.
We _____ the horse.

A linking verb joins the subject of a sentence with a word describing the subject. Two common linking verbs are "be" (in all its forms: am, are, is, be, been, was, were, etc.) and "seem."
    Examples: I am happy. You seem tired.

Because there are only a few linking verbs, frames for experimenting with linking verbs are reversed. They include the linking verbs and leave out the words to be linked:

Our family is _____.

_____ seems sad.

_____ are _____.

Verbs indicate when actions will occur. Six common tenses are:

Simple present: I smile.
Continuing present: I am smiling.
Simple (Specific) past: I smiled (yesterday).
Indeterminate past: I have smiled (at some time or other).
Continuing past: I was smiling (when something else happened).
Future: I will smile.

It's easy to create frames for tenses:

Simple past tense: Yesterday, I _____.
Indeterminate past: I have often _____.
Future: Someday you will _____.

Sample Frames

Adverbs

Adverbs tell how, when, or where an action was carried out.
> Example: The dog barked angrily yesterday.

Most adverbs end in ly: eagerly, neatly, quietly.

Our friends talked _____.
The movie ended _____.
We _____ ate dinner.

A few adverbs can add meaning to adjectives.
> Examples: I am really eager. She is less happy today.

Prepositions

Prepositions are words that indicate position or relationship.
> Examples: My hand is on top. The car is in the garage.

Usually, prepositions are found with nouns or noun phrases (adjective + noun). The result is called a prepositional phrase.
> Examples:
> after lunch
> near the wall
> on the back burner
> over the rainbow

There are only about a dozen common prepositions: around, at, by, from, in, into, near, of, on, over, to, and under. Thus, the most useful frame practice for this part of speech requires presenting the preposition and having the students complete the prepositional phrase:

> I found it on _____.
> The idea came from _____.

IRREGULAR NOUNS

Most nouns form the plural by adding s to the singular form. There are several regular "exceptions."

• If the noun ends in s, sh, ch, x, or z, add es if the plural pronunciation requires an additional syllable:
>   box, boxes; lunch, lunches

• If the noun ends in a consonant + y, change the y to i and add es:
>   army, armies; party, parties

• If the noun ends in o, add s except for: buffaloes, desperadoes, dominoes, echoes, embargoes, haloes, heroes, mosquitoes, mottoes, noes, potatoes, tomatoes, torpedoes, tornadoes, vetoes, volcanoes.

The following nouns have irregular plural forms:

singular	plural
aircraft	aircraft
calf	calves
child	children
corps	corps
deer	deer
elf	elves
fish	fish
foot	feet
goose	geese
half	halves
knife	knives
loaf	loaves
louse	lice
man	men
moose	moose
mouse	mice
sheep	sheep
thief	thieves
tooth	teeth
wife	wives
woman	women

Irregular Verbs

Most verbs form the past tense and the past particle simply by adding ed. For example:

> I shop. I shopped. I have shopped.

The following are exceptions:

present	past	past participle
am	was	been
arise	arose	arisen
awake	awoke	awaked
bear	bore	borne
beat	beat	beaten
bend	bent	bent
begin	began	begun
bleed	bled	bled
blow	blew	blown
break	broke	broken
bring	brought	brought
buy	bought	bought
catch	caught	caught
choose	chose	chosen
cling	clung	clung
come	came	come
dig	dug	dug
dive	dived	dived
do	did	done
draw	drew	drawn
drink	drank	drunk
drive	drove	driven
eat	ate	eaten
fall	fell	fallen
feel	felt	felt
fight	fought	fought
fly	flew	flown
forbid	forbade	forbidden
forget	forgot	forgotten
freeze	froze	frozen
get	got	got
go	went	gone
grow	grew	grown
hang	hung	hung

Irregular Verbs

hang (punish)	hanged	hanged
have	had	had
hear	heard	heard
hide	hid	hidden
hurt	hurt	hurt
keep	kept	kept
know	knew	known
lead	led	led
leave	left	left
lie	lay	lain
lose	lost	lost
pay	paid	paid
ring	rang	rung
run	ran	run
say	said	said
seek	sought	sought
see	saw	seen
set	set	set
shake	shook	shaken
shoot	shot	shot
shrink	shrank	shrunk
sing	sang	sung
sit	sat	sat
sleep	slept	slept
speak	spoke	spoken
spend	spent	spent
steal	stole	stolen
stick	stuck	stuck
sting	stung	stung
swear	swore	sworn
swim	swam	swum
take	took	taken
teach	taught	taught
tear	tore	torn
think	thought	thought
throw	threw	thrown
wear	wore	worn
win	won	won
wring	wrung	wrung
write	wrote	written

SENTENCE PATTERNS

Most sentences fit into three large categories: simple sentences, compound sentences, and complex sentences.

Each of these categories contains a handful of recurring patterns—about a dozen patterns in all. By familiarizing young writers with these patterns or forms, we increase the odds that they can write with clarity, precision, and variety. Below, each pattern is labeled with "P" and a number.

Simple Sentences

A simple sentence consists of a subject and a predicate. For example:
> She studies.

A simple sentence can have a plural subject:
> The two boys laughed.
> Jack and Jill went up the hill.

Likewise, a simple sentence can have a multiple verb:
> They laughed and cried.

Still, it's a *simple* sentence if the subject and the predicate work together as a unit to tell one story.

There are an infinite number of simple sentences, but most fit into one of the following generic forms:

P1: Subject + verb
> I sang.
> Jack and Jill went up the hill.

P2: Helping verb + subject + verb [question sentences]
> Are you eating?
> Could she smile?

P3: Subject + verb + direct object
> I found an elephant.
> She hit a home run.

Sentence Patterns

P4: Subject + verb + indirect object

    I smiled at my friend.

P5: Subject + linking verb + adjective

    I am happy.

    You seem confused.

P6: Subject + linking verb + noun phrase

    I am a teacher.

    Teaching is hard work.

P7: Implied subject + verb [imperative or command]

    Eat. (Understood: "You eat.")

    Go away.

Compound Sentences

A compound sentence consists of two or more simple sentences, usually joined by coordinating conjunctions (and, but, or) or by semicolons.

P8: Simple sentence + coordinating conjunction + simple sentence

    I smile, and you smile.

    I smile, but you cry.

    I'll study, or I'll go swimming.

P9: Simple sentence + semicolon + simple sentence

    She likes to dance; she does it with style.

Complex Sentences

Complex sentences consist of a simple or a compound sentence plus one or more subordinate clauses (also called "dependent clauses"). A subordinate clause contains a subject and predicate but feels incomplete until joined to a sentence. These clauses usually begin with a subordinating conjunction such as although, because, if, and when, or with a relative pronoun such as that or which. Examples of subordinate clauses are:

    When it's raining...

    If they need help...

Sentence Patterns

Complex sentences often take the following forms:

P10: Subordinate clause + simple sentence
>   Although we're friends, we sometimes disagree.
>   If you smile, I'll be happy.
>   When I work hard, I get things done.

P11: Simple sentence + subordinate clause
>   We sometimes disagree although we're friends.
>   I want to eat now because I'm hungry.
>   No one was laughing until you came.

P12: Simple sentence + "that" or "which" clause
>   I want to read the book that you read.
>   This is the door which must stay open.

P13: Simple sentence + "who" or "what" clause
>   I don't care who is going.
>   She never learned what you do.

P14: Subject of sentence + "who" or "what" clause + predicate
>   The red house, which burned down, belonged to my friend.

Sentence Fragments

A sentence fragment is a word or word group lacking a subject or a predicate.

P15: Single words, often interjections
>   Hey.
>   No.
>   Why?

P16: Phrases and dependent clauses
>   Never again.
>   Because I said so.

A sentence fragment can cause confusion if the reader expects a complete sentence. However, fragments are often used success-fully in dialogue.

DIAGRAMMING SENTENCES

Too much of a good thing is usually a bad thing. Diagramming sentences is an unfortunate example. In the past, this handy analytical tool has been overdone, but in moderation it can clarify sentence structure. To help students identify the elements of the sentence and how these parts work together, you don't need complex schemes. The simple label-and-arrow method works fine.

DIRECTIONS:
1. On the board, write an example of the type of sentence you want students to study. In the beginning, use very simple sentences.
2. Label the parts and draw the arrows as illustrated below. The arrows indicate the relationship between words and phrases.
3. Discuss the reasons for each arrow. For example, in sentence A, "very" does not refer to "batter" but to "tall." In sentence B, the adjectives "red," "white," and "blue," though located in the predicate, refer back to the subject.

   In some cases, there may be legitimate debate about the relationships between the words. What's most important is that students begin to think about the parts.
4. Give students similar sentences to diagram. In the beginning, you might list the elements to label, for example: the subject, the verb, and the direct object.

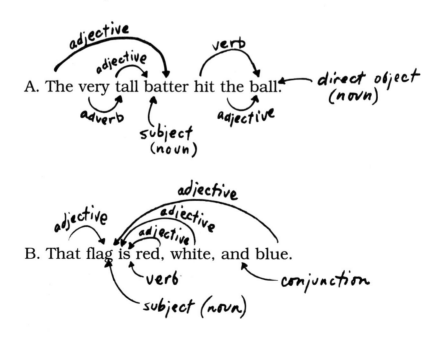

SAMPLE SAYINGS

A rolling stone gathers no moss.

A stitch in time saves nine.

Actions speak louder than words.

After the ship has sunk, everyone knows how it might have been saved.

An apple a day keeps the doctor away.

Be grateful for luck, but don't depend on it.

Better ask twice than go wrong once.

Birds of a feather flock together.

Do not bite the hand that feeds you.

Do not put off until tomorrow what you can do today.

Do not throw the arrow which will return against you.

Don't fall before you're pushed.

Don't open a shop unless you know how to smile.

Eat to live, not live to eat.

Fish or cut bait.

If at first you don't succeed, try, try again.

If there is no wind, row.

If you have knowledge, let others light their candles at it.

If you lie down with dogs, you'll rise up with fleas.

If you want enemies, lend money to your friends.

The grass is always greener on the other side of the fence.

Keep cool; anger is not an argument.

Keep your eyes on the stars, and your feet on the ground.

Keep your fears to yourself, but share your courage with others.

Know how to do good a little at a time, and often.

Learn as much by writing as by reading.

Learn to love good books.

Let sleeping dogs lie.

Let us help one another.

Love truth, and pardon error.

Measure a thousand times and cut once.

Never give advice unless asked.

Never promise more than you can do.

Never spend your money before you have it.

Seize the day.

The only way to have a friend is to be one.

When fate hands us a lemon, let us try to make lemonade.

When in doubt, tell the truth.

TEACHING ESL

If you've studied a second language, you know that language patterns are often more arbitrary than logical (I go, I went, I have gone). That's why mastery requires lots of practice. When working with English as Second Language (ESL) students, the most important strategy may be: Patience!

Read aloud to students on a regular basis. The ear is a powerful ally for mastering usage, sentence patterns, punctuation, vocabulary, and other elements of language.
• Read from a variety of sources: fiction and nonfiction books, newspapers, advertisements, jokes, comics, and letters. Don't overlook picture books. Classics by Dr. Seuss and other masters have been used successfully even at the college level.
• Watch the pace. Reading slightly slower than normal may help students follow the text.
• Keep reading sessions short. A dramatic five-minute reading can accomplish a great deal.
• Stop occasionally to reinforce a concept. For example, if you've been teaching prepositional phrases and notice an interesting one while reading, write it on the board and discuss it.

Have students read aloud in small groups. You can also use oral reading to illustrate concepts taught analytically. For example, if students are having trouble determining when to use "a," "an," and "the," you might prepare a read-aloud text filled with these words.

Do focused practices. If students have a hard time with the simple past tense, give them a story in the simple present, underline each verb, and have them rewrite every verb in the past. Athletic coaches have long used this "overlearning" technique, and it's just as effective in language class.

Allow extra time for the toughest problems. For example, while the difference between "a car" and "the car" may seem obvious to a native speaker, this distinction is tricky for ESL students whose language doesn't use articles. Likewise, because some languages don't change the verb to indicate past tense, students may persist in saying "Yesterday, I eat lunch" because that usage sounds correct.